# NAHUM DANSULE

# MORE THAN THE COAT

## THE JOSEPH ANOINTING

ISBN(Paperback): 978-978-59961-6-6
ISBN(eBook): 978-978-59961-7-3

Published by:
**Cheret Creative Company**
*Lifecenta*, Yopet Oil Building, Adegbayi,
New Ife Road, Ibadan, Oyo State, Nigeria.
T: +234 803 095 7661
E: hello@cheretcreatives.com, cheretpublishing@gmail.com
W: www.cheretcreatives.com
*Facebook/Twitter/Instagram/LinkedIn/Google*: @CheretCreatives

The Author can be reached at:
Salvation for All Nations Ministry International
City of David, P.O.Box 518 Wukari,
Taraba State, Nigeria. West Africa.
Email:sfanmi.programs@gmail.com
Tel: +2349075033829

Cover Image: Getty Images



*All Scriptures are taken from the Authorized King James Version (AKJV) of the Holy Bible unless quoted otherwise.*

*Text set in Arno Pro and Ruda*
*Printed in the Federal Republic of Nigeria*

# Dedication

This book is dedicated to my beloved Dad, **Habila Danjuma Sule**, of blessed memory.

He fought the good fight of faith and has ventured on to a higher plane in Christ Jesus. He was a huge source of encouragement to the ministry and me; a mighty man of wisdom, a father, and a grandfather.

# Contents


| | | |
|---|---|---|
| *Introduction* | | 1 |
| Chapter One: | **The Lord Was With Him** | 3 |
| Chapter Two: | **He Was Industrious** | 7 |
| Chapter Three: | **Joseph Dreamed A Dream** | 11 |
| Chapter Four: | **Supernatural Grace** | 17 |
| *Conclusion* | | 21 |

# Introduction

***More Than The Coat*** – *the Joseph Anointing* was born out of my daily study of the Word of God. Each day, I would study five chapters of the Bible as morning devotion. This book is to encourage Christians to trust the Almighty God for the kind of faith, patience, and tolerance that Joseph engaged, to obtain the anointing of royalty.

The anointing on Joseph is such an awesome and dynamic kind of grace that is needed for such a time as this. When you desire and develop the hunger to save lives, it becomes God's desire for you to be anointed in this manner. Unfortunately, families, cities, and nations are perishing because of the scarcity of people with big dreams or vision that rests on the well-being of other people.

Certainly, we would see changes in our churches, homes, businesses, and political spheres if and when we become the JOSEPH of our generations. You can discover a lot on a scenic route. Indeed, God allows His anointing to rest on anybody that is adventurous enough and ready to take the journey because His anointing is available for all.

Joseph, Nehemiah, and Daniel, to mention a few, paid the price to obtain grace and the anointing of God upon their lives. Your dreams or vision will usher you into your next level and dimension in God, if you are willing to pay the price. It may take a long time for the fulfillment of your dreams or vision; but, wait for the appointed time.

> *"For the vision is yet for an appointed time, but at the end, it shall speak, and not lie: though it tarry, wait for it; because it will surely come, it will not tarry."*
> *Habakkuk 2:3*

# CHAPTER ONE

# The LORD was with Him

*"And the LORD was with Joseph, and he was a PROSPEROUS man, and he was in the house of his master the Egyptian. And his master saw that the LORD was with him, and that the LORD made all that he did to PROSPER in his hand. And Joseph found grace in his sight, and he served him: and he made him overseer over his house, and all that he had he put into his hand."* Genesis 39:2 – 4 KJV

Faithfulness to God guarantees His divine favor, grace, and anointing. Surely, God prospers anyone who prioritises Him, as Joseph did. It may be that the affairs of Potiphar's family had remarkably gone backward before the arrival of Joseph; but, upon Joseph's coming, it took on a new look. This meant that on Joseph's arrival into Potiphar's family, a particular BLESSING of heaven attended him. This is nothing else but what I would call the JOSEPH ANOINTING.

*"And it came to pass, when Joseph was come unto his brethren, that they stript Joseph out of his coat, his coat of many colours that was on him; . . ."*
Genesis 37:23 KJV

Joseph had the Spirit of wisdom and special GRACE in him, which cannot be taken away by anyone - the *Joseph Anointing*. The anointing resides inside him, not outside; therefore, Joseph had that which could not be taken away from him. His brothers stripped him of his coat of many colours, but they could not strip him of his VIRTUE and

PRUDENCE.

*"Who shall separate us from the love of Christ?*
*Shall tribulation, or distress, or persecution, or*
*famine, or nakedness, or peril, or sword?"*
Romans 8:35 KJV

People can separate us from friends and loved ones, but they cannot deprive us of the GRACIOUS PRESENCE of our God. When Joseph had no friends, and none of his relations were with him, his God remained with him.

While Joseph was separated from his family and friends, in the house of the Egyptian, the presence of the LORD with him was enough; He comforted him.

You must develop a hunger for knowing the LORD in every area of your life before this anointing would become operational in your life. Your obedience, devotion, and commitment to God's kingdom causes would grant you the *Joseph Anointing*.

*"If they obey and serve him,*
*they shall spend their days in prosperity, and their*
*years in pleasures."* Job 36:11 KJV

As you focus on Jesus, prepare for the *Joseph Anointing* to be released upon your life as the Almighty God reveals Himself through you.

*"To shew that the LORD is upright:*
*He is my rock, and there is no unrighteousness in*
*him."* Psalms 92:15 KJV

CHAPTER TWO

# He was Industrious

> *"And the LORD was with Joseph, and he was a PROSPEROUS man; and he was in the house of his master the Egyptian."* Genesis 39:2 KJV

It is God's presence with us that makes all we do prosperous; therefore, those that would prosper and be successful in life and destiny must make a habit of giving God the PRAISE for all that is to be done or done already. Joseph's master preferred him above others, so much so that he made him the steward of his household. Because of his honesty and industrious capability, his master's household prospered as he was rising and thriving.

> *"And the man Jeroboam was a mighty man of valour: and Solomon seeing the young man that he was INDUSTRIOUS, he made him ruler over all the charge of the house of Joseph."* 1 Kings 11:28 KJV

The Bible says,
> *"Seest thou a man prudent and faithful, and diligent in his business? He shall stand before kings at length and not always before mean men."* Proverbs 22:29

It is the wisdom of those that are in any sort of authority to countenance and employ those it appears that the presence of God is with.

*"Mine eyes shall be upon the faithful of the land, that
they may dwell with me:
he that walketh in a perfect way, he shall serve me."*
Psalms 101:6 KJV

Potiphar knew that putting all of his households in Joseph's
hands will attract more PROSPERITY than in his hand. He
that is faithful in a few things stands fair for being made ruler
over many things.

*"His lord said unto him, well done, thou good and
faithful servant: thou hast been faithful over a few
things, I will make thee ruler over many things: enter
thou into the joy of thy lord."*
Matthew 25:21 KJV

God favored his master for his sake, He BLESSED the
Egyptian's house for Joseph's sake. It is possible to contact
the *Joseph Anointing* that can change you and the people
around you for good.

# CHAPTER THREE

# Joseph Dreamed a Dream

*"And Joseph dreamed a dream, and he told it his brethren: and they hated him yet the more. And he said unto them, Hear, I pray you, this dream which I have dreamed. For behold, we were binding sheaves in the field, and, lo, my sheaf arose, and also stood upright; and behold, your sheaves stood round about, and make obeisance to my sheaf."*
Genesis 37:5 – 7 KJV

In the *Joseph Anointing*, the blessings are usually to be manifested in the future, not in the immediate. Therefore, it is vital to pay attention and focus on every dream that you dreamed of because your dreams are the pictures of what you will become in the future. Do not worry about those that will hate you when you share your dreams and visions with them.

*"And Joseph dreamed a dream, and he told it his brethren: and they hated him yet the more."*
Genesis 37:5 KJV

These are his blood brothers that hated him the more just because he shared his dreams and visions with them. The *Joseph Anointing* is a very high-level anointing that will show you how your latter end in life will be; therefore. You must also be very careful with whom you share your dreams and visions.

*"A man's enemies will be the members of his own household."* Mathew 10:36 NIV

In sharing with his brothers, he thought they would pray and support the dreams to become reality; instead, they hated him and wanted to terminate and abort the dreams and visions.

Without a doubt, Joseph's dream was a big one, such that even his father rebuked him because of the size of the dream. As you are reading this book today, what is your dream? Do you have a dream? How big is your dream?

*"And he told it to his father, and to his brethren: and his father rebuked him, and said unto him, what is this dream that thou hast dreamed? Shall I and thy mother and thy brethren indeed come bow down ourselves to thee to the earth?"* Genesis 37:10 KJV

The *Joseph Anointing* is for all believers, who have accepted the Lord Jesus Christ as their Lord and Savior, not for those who intend to use it for their personal gain. To receive this anointing, maturity and commitment to God and His kingdom are the requirements; they enable this dimension of the anointing of God.

You must have a large heart that can accommodate others, even those that hurt you, in the process of manifesting your dream or vision.

> *"Now therefore be not grieved, nor angry with yourselves, that ye sold me hither: for God did send me before you to preserve life."* Genesis 45:5 KJV

The *Joseph Anointing* preserves life. One man's dream and vision saved almost all the nations of the world from a grievous famine that could have terminated so many lives. Your dream or vision will save your generation, your community, your country, and the world at large. The *Joseph Anointing* is hanging in the balance, are you ready for it? It is time to save your entire generation from perishing for lack of vision.

> *"Where there is no vision, the people perish: but he that keepeth the law, happy is he."*
> Proverbs 29:18 KJV

> *"And when they saw him afar off, they conspired against him to slay him. And they said one to another, Behold, this dreamer cometh. Come now therefore, and let us slay him, and cast him into some pit, and we will say, Some evil beast hath devoured him: and we shall see what will become of his dreams."*
> Genesis 37:19 -20 KJV

The enemy knows that your dreams and visions will terminate poverty, sicknesses, diseases, stagnation, infirmities, and satan's stronghold in the life and destiny of countless people. So, your dreams and visions set you up to become his number one enemy. You must always pray that the Almighty GOD sustains you, your dreams, and your visions by His grace; if not, the devil, the killer of dreams and visions, may abort your mandate.

The anointing empowered Joseph with a special GRACE that enabled him to overcome every challenge and attack that arose to stop and abort his dreams and visions.

*"And it come to pass, when Joseph was come unto his brethren, that they stript Joseph out of his coat, his coat of many colours that was on him."*
Genesis 37:23 KJV

With this understanding, you can boldly say that "The anointing is not in the coat of many colours, which I love; instead, it resides inside of me. It is a deposit from God! You can strip me of everything else in life, but as long as there is still breath in me, I will manifest the *Joseph Anointing*."

This anointing is fresh oil from God. The throne of grace is open for everyone, who will approach to obtain mercy and find grace in this time of need. I believe you need this anointing to manifest the miraculous in your affairs.

*"Let us therefore come boldly unto the throne of grace that we may obtain mercy, and find grace to help in time of need."* Hebrews 4:16

If you are willing and obedient, the LORD will empower you with the *Joseph Anointing* that lifts one's head above his or her equals.

> *"But my horn shalt thou exalt like the horn of an unicorn: I shall be anointed with fresh oil."*
> Psalms 92:10

# CHAPTER FOUR

# Supernatural Grace

*"And it came to pass from the time that he had made him overseer in his house, and over all that he had, that the LORD BLESSED the Egyptian's house for Joseph's sake; and the blessing of the LORD was upon all that he had in the house, and in the field."*
Genesis 39:5 KJV

When the *Joseph Anointing* rests upon a man or woman of God, it comes with the following SUPERNATURAL GRACE:

## 1. Prosperity

*"And the LORD was with Joseph, and he was a PROSPEROUS man; and he was in the house of his master the Egyptian. And his master saw that the LORD was with him, and that the LORD made all that he did to PROSPER in his hand."*
Genesis 39:2 – 3 KJV

## 2. Blessing

*"And it came to pass from the time that he had made him overseer in his house, and over all that he had, that the LORD BLESSED the Egyptian's house for Joseph's sake; and the 3. BLESSING of the LORD was upon all that he had in the house, and in the field." Genesis 39:5* KJV

## 3. Grace to Overcome Sin

*"And it came to pass after these things, that his*

*master's wife cast her eyes upon Joseph; and she said, LIE WITH ME. But he REFUSED, and said unto his master's wife, Behold, my master wotteth not what is with me in the house, and he hath committed all that he hath to my hand; There is none greater in this house than I; neither hath he kept back any thing from me but thee, because thou art his wife: how than can I do this great wickedness, and SIN against God?"*
Genesis 39:8 – 9 KJV

### 4. Grace to Overcome Every Prison in Life

*"And Joseph's master took him, and put him into the prison, a place where the king's prisoners were bound: and he was there in prison."* Genesis 39:20) KJV

### 5. Favor

*"But the LORD was with Joseph, and shewed him mercy, and gave him FAVOR in the sight of the keeper of the prison."*
Genesis 39:21 KJV

### 6. Dominion

*"And the keeper of the prison committed to Joseph's hand all the prisoners that were in the prison; and whatsoever they did there, he was the doer of it. The keeper of the prison looked not to anything that was under his hand; because the LORD was with him, and that which he did, the LORD made it to prosper."*
Genesis 39:22 - 23 KJV

## 7. Interpretation of Dreams

*"And Joseph answered and said, This is the interpretation thereof: the three baskets are three days: Yet within three days shall Pharaoh lift up thy head from off thee, and shall hang thee on a tree, and the birds shall eat thy flesh from off thee."*
Genesis 40:18 – 119 KJV

## 8. Promotion

*"Thou shalt be over my house, and according unto thy word shall all my people be ruled: only in the throne will I be greater than thou. And Pharaoh said unto Joseph, see, I have set thee over all the land of Egypt."*
Genesis 41:40 – 41 KJV

Get on your knees and pray this prayer:
*"O Lord my God, empower me with the Joseph Anointing so that I may evangelize my entire family, community, country, and nations of the world for you. This I pray, in Jesus' mighty name. Amen."*

# Conclusion

To move higher in life, you must surround yourself with people that are smarter than you, your dreams, or your visions. This will empower you to preserve life.

The size of your dream or vision determines how great you become in life and destiny. Creation is waiting for the manifestation of your dreams or visions; remember, where there is no vision, the people perish.

*"Where there is no vision. The people perish: but he that keepeth the law, happy is he."* Proverbs 29:18

# Notes

Do you have personal visions and dreams; for which you are setting goals? Here are a few pages to document them.